The WIDOW'S OFFERING

Mark 12:41–44;
Luke 21:1–4 for children

Written by Joanne Bader
Illustrated by Pamela Johnson

CONCORDIA PUBLISHING HOUSE · SAINT LOUIS

D1360463

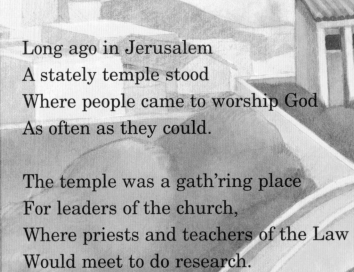

Long ago in Jerusalem
A stately temple stood
Where people came to worship God
As often as they could.

The temple was a gath'ring place
For leaders of the church,
Where priests and teachers of the Law
Would meet to do research.

They wanted to know everything
About the Word of God.
So they discussed and studied it,
But their thoughts were sometimes flawed.

Now Jesus sometimes went there too.
He'd teach and preach the Word.
And many listened as He spoke.
Some trusted what they heard.

One day when Jesus visited
The temple that was there,
He talked with scribes and Pharisees
And spent time in prayer.

As He sat, He looked around.
He saw a certain space
That was quite near the treasury.
It was the off'ring place.

Special containers were lined up
All in a nice neat row.
The people put their money in—
Their gift to God, you know.

He watched as rich folks walked on by
And put in larger amounts.
They had more cash where that came from
In other big accounts.

And then a widow lady came
With copper coins, just two.
She dropped them in—that's all she had,
For she was poor, 'twas true.

When Jesus saw what she had giv'n—
Less than a penny's worth—
He knew she had given all
She had here on this earth.

He called to His disciples then.
He turned and said aloud,
"This widow, poor, has given more
Than others in the crowd.

"For some have made no sacrifice.
They have lots more to spare.
The widow lady standing there
Has no more coins to share."

This story shows what our God thinks
About the gifts we bring
To help our church and missions, too,
To honor Christ the King.

Our gifts are how we worship Him,
Just like we sing and pray.
Our gifts are how we show our love
To Jesus every day.

You see the most important thing
Is not how much we give,
But how we feel deep in our hearts—
Does our faith really live?

Dear Father God, please bless our gifts,
However big or small.
Use them to build Your Church on earth
And share Christ's love for all.

Dear Parents,

This familiar story of the widow's offering emphasizes the love and trust of the giver rather than the size of the gift. The poor woman was willing to sacrifice all she had because she had faith that God would supply all she needed to support her body and life. Her offering truly came from her heart.

This Bible story is often used to teach us how to give, what we call stewardship. Sometimes we think of our offering as money only. However, our gifts can also be serving our church and community with our talents and our time. As Jesus says in this Bible story, it is the faith and love in the heart that is important—not the kind of talent or the amount given. All that we have and are is a gift from God (Psalm 24:1). Our offerings of time, talent, and treasure, given in love, are our gifts back to Him for His profound gift to us, that is, His very life on the cross for the forgiveness of our sins. The Lord blesses these offerings and works through them to spread His love and His Word in His kingdom on earth.

Giving is a personal choice, a natural response. The woman in this story was so moved to give and so confident in her faith that she gave all she had. We can have the same confidence in our own giving: "Remember this: Whoever . . . sows generously will also reap generously. Each man should give what he has decided in his heart to give, not reluctantly or under compulsion, for God loves a cheerful giver. And God is able to make all grace abound to you, so that in all things at all times, having all that you need, you will abound in every good work" (2 Corinthians 9:6–8).

Talk with your family about ways you can give back to God. Some ideas to consider are contributing to a missionary family or seminary student or volunteering at your community food bank. Whatever you decide to do, do it joyfully and with the assurance of God's blessings through Jesus Christ.

To Him be the glory!

The Editor